DISCOVERING YOUR PURPOSE

KEYS TO UNLOCKING YOUR DIVINE PURPOSE

BY

INNOCENT T. MATURA

Copyright © 2018 by Innocent T. Matura

All rights reserved. No part of this book may be reproduced or transmitted in any form or by any means without written permission of the author.

ISBN: 978-0-7974-9102-1

For more information: **pastormatura@gmail.com**

Dedication

This book is dedicated to my parents Majors Solomon and Netsai Matura. I am forever grateful for your love and sacrifice by providing and giving me the best opportunities in life from your limited resources. You have modeled a life dedicated to serving God and raised me in the ways of God. I am thankful for your prayers and for allowing me to pursue my divine purpose.

Acknowledgements

I would like to acknowledge the following people who impacted my life towards fulfilling my divine purpose:

- Bishop Colin and Senior Reverend Dr. Sarah Nyathi, my spiritual parents. Thank you for your obedience to God and for being visionaries. It has given me room to fulfill my divine purpose.
- Noniah Matura my beautiful, bold and brilliant wife, thank you for your love and support. Serving God with you is a great joy and blessing.
- Reverend CS Tuturu, an outstanding servant of God. Thank you for obeying the Voice of God. Your mentorship and training has aligned me with my divine purpose.
- Reverend T Mupamhanga, you are truly a blessing and an inspiration to me. Thank you for guiding me through the process of writing my first book.
- All the Pastors, Elders, Departmental leaders and saints of Harvest House International Church who I serve with in God's vineyard. Special mention to HHI Pretoria

saints, HHI East London saints, HHI Midrand saints and HHI RSA Hub. You are a blessing.
- All the Officers and saints of The Salvation Army that I worked with, it was a great joy. Those years laid a strong foundation for my spiritual life and ministry. Special mention to the Salvation Army Student Fellowship MSU and Prayer Builders, what a blessing it was seeking God together for revival.
- All the brothers and sisters from MSU Christian Union, whom I served and fellowshipped with. Those years of evangelizing in schools and rural areas were great preparation for discovering and fulfilling my divine purpose.
- All the brothers and friends from Mazowe High School Scripture Union. It was a joy sharing the early years of my spiritual journey with you.
- Thenjie Ndlovu your hard work and efforts on this book are well appreciated.
- Stephanie and Joshua you are a wonderful blessing to my life, I love you.

John 1:22-23

"*So they said to him, "**Who are you?** We need to give an answer to those who sent us. What do you say about yourself?" He said,* **"I am the voice of one crying out in the wilderness, 'Make straight the way of the Lord,'** *as the prophet Isaiah said."*
(ESV)

Esther 4:14

"For if you keep silent at this time, relief and deliverance will rise for the Jews from another place, but you and your father's house will perish. **And who knows whether you have not come to the kingdom for such a time as this?**"
(ESV)

Act 13:36

"For David, after he had served **the purpose of God in his own generation***, fell asleep and was laid with his fathers and saw corruption,"(ESV)*

FOREWORD

There is nothing as gratifying and fulfilling in life as knowing that you are walking in the will and the purposes of God. Locked within every individual is great purpose that will bring tremendous fulfillment and meaning to life when pursued with understanding, wisdom and knowledge.

In this classic book, Discovering Your Purpose, Innocent Matura presents in simplicity the importance of purpose in every person's life. The book outlines great insights on how to unlock your divine purpose in a practical way. There are gifts and callings that God has placed in every individual which are powerful tools that will ensure that you fulfill your purposes. Senior Pastor I. Matura explains how you can discover your gifts and calling in a profound way. He then further expounds on other key elements of fulfilling purpose which include discovering your talents, passion and place of assignment.

This book will challenge anyone who wants to fulfill God's purpose in life. It is a must read for anyone who wants to understand how to walk the journey of fulfilling God's will for their lives.

Reverend T. Mupamhanga

TABLE OF CONTENTS

Dedication...3
Acknowledgments...5
Foreword..9
Preface...13
Introduction...17

Chapters:

One: Understanding the meaning & qualities of purpose..21

Two: Discover the mind of God...............................35

Three: Discover your calling and gifts....................45

Four: Discover your talents 61

Five: Discover your passion....................................69

Six: Discover your place...77

Seven: Purpose led life..89

TABLE OF CONTENTS

PREFACE

I believe life begins when you discover why you were born. From a young age I had a desire to understand the reason why I was born. As long as I can remember I always had a strong sense that there was more to life than I knew. Those early years when I was in primary school were the beginning of my search for purpose. It was the beginning of a lifelong journey.

I remember just before I wrote my Grade Seven final exams, my father sat me down and asked me what I wanted do when I grow up. I do not remember what I said exactly but I expressed my desire to pass my exams, go to high school and then go to university. My dad encouraged me that if I worked hard and avoided being distracted by worthless things like alcohol, I could achieve it. He advised me to maximize the opportunity I had that he never had to go further with his education.

High School was a time of growing up and self-discovery, in the midst of dealing with peer pressure. The words of advice from my parents preserved me during my teenage years. I was learning new things that caught my interest. I took up Technical Graphics as one of my practical subjects, I liked it and it aroused the desire to pursue it as career. Unfortunately when I got to Form three there was no teacher for Technical Graphics, so I could not pursue it further. At this point I discovered I was good at commercial subjects, so after I passed my O- Levels I chose to do a pure commercial combination at A-Level (Accounts, Economics and Management of Business). Although I had chosen a career path, I was still searching to understand my purpose in life.

During my final year in A-Level I had an experience that would transform my life forever. One morning, I was sitting in our school hall during the weekly Sunday service. The visiting speaker who was a former Head boy at Mazowe High School, now an elderly married man is his sixties; was preaching from Genesis 1 verse 1 to 3. As he spoke, my whole life passed before me in a moment, I saw how confused and meaningless my life was. Concluding his sermon he made an invitation for those who wanted to receive Jesus Christ to stand up; I stood without hesitation to pray the prayer to receive Jesus Christ as my Savior and Lord. This was not the first time I prayed this prayer but this time it was different and my life was transformed. I had always attended church services growing up in a Christian home, it was the law that Sunday we all go to church as a family. Going to church was a tradition I grew up following but I had never made a conscious decision to receive Jesus and be born again.

This salvation and new birth experience brought new meaning to my life. These were the days before email and Whatsapp, so I wrote to my mother a letter narrating the whole experience. I saw everything with a new perspective and I had a passionate desire to share my experience with as many people as possible. I began to read the Bible with a refreshed passion. So often l would read late into the night. The word of God became real to me and I began to understand it better. I now had a strong desire to serve God.

I passed my A Levels and got a place to study a degree in

Accounting at a local university in Gweru. It was at the university that my journey to discover my purpose began to take shape. I read a lot of Christian books, one of the books that made a great impact on me; 'Understanding Your Potential' written by Dr. Myles Munroe. It inspired me to make a conscious decision to work towards discovering my purpose in life and maximize my divine potential.

I will share some of my experiences in the journey to discovering my purpose throughout this book. My desire is that the keys from the word of God and a few of my personal experiences will help you the reader discover your purpose in life.

In His service,
I.T. Matura
17/12/17

INTRODUCTION

It is important to understand that God is a God of purpose. Everything that God created has a specific purpose. Nothing existed by chance; it has all been purposefully created by God.

Genesis 1:14
"And God said, "Let there be lights in the expanse of the heavens to separate the day from the night. And let them be for signs and for seasons, and for days and years,"
(ESV)

Have you considered that even things that look small and insignificant like flies have a purpose? If a fly has a purpose, then you definitely have a purpose in this life. God created man to fulfill a general and a specific purpose. The general purpose is to manage God's creation and to please Him. The specific purpose is one's divine life assignment and takes one to make an effort to discover it personally. It's a journey to discover how to please God with your life.

Genesis 1:26

*"Then God said, "Let us make man in **our image**, after **our likeness**. And let them **have dominion** over the fish of the sea and over the birds of the heavens and over the livestock and over all the earth and over every creeping thing that creeps on the earth."*
(ESV)

Everyone is created to fulfill a destined purpose. Adam was the first man created and God outlined to him his purpose. Adam was aware of the purpose, why God had created and placed him in the garden. God instructed him to manage the Garden of Eden.

Genesis 2:15

*"The Lord God took the man and put him in the garden of Eden to **work it and keep it**."*
(ESV)

When we don't know our purpose, life does not make sense. Life begins when you discover your purpose, the reason why you were born. It is critical that one discovers and fulfills their divine purpose. In chapter one I explore the meaning and the qualities of purpose. Incorporating the rest of the chapters, I will expound on the following keys that will help you unlock your divine purpose:

I. Discover the mind of God
II. Discover your calling and gifts
III. Discover your abilities and talents
IV. Discover your passion
V. Discover your place

In the last chapter I look at how we can live a purpose-led life. Let's travel together on a journey through this book to unlocking your divine purpose.

CHAPTER ONE
UNDERSTANDING THE MEANING AND QUALITIES OF PURPOSE

Act 13:36
*"For David, after he had served the **purpose of God** in his own generation, fell asleep and was laid with his fathers and saw corruption,"*
(ESV)

It is critical to understand the meaning of purpose. This will help you to know what you are looking for. You cannot find or discover something if you do not know what you are looking for. Understanding the meaning of purpose will help us on the journey to discover it.

DEFINING PURPOSE

I. Purpose is the reason for being

It is the reason why you exist or were born. Your birth was not by chance or a mistake, people might say you are a mistake but with God you are a masterpiece.

You are not here on earth by default but by design. God planned your existence way before you were born. Your existence has been designed by God.

Jeremiah 1:5
*"Before **I formed you** in the womb **I knew you**,*
*and before you were born **I consecrated you;***
***I appointed you** a prophet to the nations."*
(ESV)

II. Purpose is the primary use of something/someone

Everything is created or designed for a certain primary use. "When you don't know the use of something abuse is inevitable" Myles Munroe. There is primary use and secondary use. For example a car's primary use is to transport from point A to point B. Its secondary use can be to play music using the car radio. If the car can longer move because of a mechanical failure but the radio is still functioning it has lost its purpose.

2 Timothy 2:20

*Now in a great house there are not only **vessels** of gold and silver but also of wood and clay, some for **honorable use**, some for dishonorable.*
(ESV)

God created everyone with a certain primary use or ability and the rest of our abilities are secondary. So your divine purpose is your primary use. When you fail to discover your purpose, you are likely to abuse yourself.

III.   Purpose is one's life assignment

Purpose is connected to your life assignment. That is the main assignment we are born to carry out. When you discover this assignment you unlock your purpose. Everything in your life will revolve around that assignment. John the Baptist was aware of his main assignment, to prepare the way for the coming of Jesus Christ. That was his purpose and he made it the key focus of his life.

John 1:22-23

*"So they said to him, "**Who are you?** We need to give an answer to those who sent us. What do you say about yourself?" 23 He said,* **"I am the voice of one crying out in the wilderness, 'Make straight the way of the Lord,'** *as the prophet Isaiah said." (ESV)*

DESTINY QUESTIONS

There are critical questions that we need to ask ourselves. I call them destiny questions because they reveal our destiny and purpose. These questions are interlinked; take time to answer them on a piece of paper. If you are not sure, give yourself time to discover the answers as you read this book.

I. **Who am I?**
- This is a question of identity
- Identity comes from the source of life, that is God
- Your identity is linked to your purpose

II. **What am I able to do?**
- This is a question of potential

- Potential is the untapped ability or power
- The potential of what we are capable of doing is determined by our purpose

III. Why am I here?
- This a question of purpose
- Purpose is the reason why you exist or you were created
- Purpose originates from the one who created you

IV. Where am I going?
- This a question of vision
- Vision is your predetermined desirable future
- Vision is birthed by your divine purpose

V. How do I get there?
- This is a question of strategy
- Strategy is the method and way to achieve your vision
- Strategy determines how to fulfill your divine purpose

VI. How will I be remembered?
- This is a question of legacy
- Legacy is the heritage and inheritance you live behind

- Your legacy is a determined by how well you live your divine purpose

VII. What will happen to me after death?
- This is a question of eternal destiny
- Eternal destiny can either be spent in heaven or in hell
- The way you live your life on earth and the choices you make, will determine your eternal destiny and reward

Apostle Paul towards the end of his life showed that he had discovered, lived and fulfilled his divine purpose. During his life he must have asked himself similar destiny questions. Knowing that he is about to die, he had no regrets; he had lived a life of purpose and was assured of his eternal destiny. Paul is a good role model to learn how to live a life of purpose.

Acts 20:24

"But I do not account my life of any value nor as precious to myself, ***if only I may finish my course and the ministry*** *that I received from the Lord Jesus, to testify to the gospel of the grace of God."*

2 Timothy 4:6-8

*"For I am already being poured out as a drink offering, and the time of my departure has come. I have **fought the good fight**, I have **finished the race**, I have **kept the faith**. Henceforth there is laid up for me the **crown of righteousness**, which the Lord, the righteous judge, will award to me on that day, and not only to me but also to all who have loved his appearing."*

QUALITIES OF PURPOSE

Purpose has certain qualities that can transform the lives of people who discover it. These qualities will help us to understand the nature and importance of purpose. The following are qualities of purpose:

1. **It gives meaning to life**

   Purpose gives you a good reason to wake up every morning. Your life is meaningful when you discover your purpose. Purpose makes you serve or work with joy and have a sense of fulfillment.

Without understanding your purpose, life is confusing and meaningless. You will just be going through the motions. The words of King Solomon are relevant when you do not understand your purpose; "meaningless, meaningless, everything is meaningless…" I know a brother who read this portion of scripture as a young high school student and was convicted to give his life to Jesus Christ. That was the beginning of the process of finding the meaning of life and discovering his purpose.

Jesus clearly understood His purpose; He was sure of the reason why He was born. That gave meaning to His life on earth and He would often tell people His purpose.

John 4:34
*"Jesus said to them, "**My food is to do the will of him who sent me and to accomplish his work.**"*
(ESV)

2. **It gives focus to life**

Purpose helps you to focus on issues that are crucial to

your destiny. When you lack purpose you will most likely be all over the place, without a clear goal in life. You are almost living a life of trial and error, which is very frustrating.

Purpose helps you to prioritize issues and activities. It declutters your life. Understanding my purpose has helped me prioritize and focus on issues that are in line with my divine purpose. That has empowered me to get rid of things that are unproductive, so as to concentrate mainly on issues related to my purpose.

Peter and the first apostles understood the importance of focusing on their purpose. When a crisis arose in the distribution of food to widows, they refused to be derailed. They determined to focus on prayer and the word, which was in line with their purpose and made a decision to assign others to distribute food.

Acts 6:4
*"But we will **devote** ourselves to **prayer and to the ministry of the word.**" (ESV)*

3. **It gives a driving force to life**

Purpose empowers and energizes you to move forward. It has ability to keep you going even when facing difficulties and challenges. It motivates you to keep moving forward on your journey of fulfilling your purpose.

Purpose driven people are passionate about what they do. Dr. John Maxwell, (whom from following and reading of his books,) I believe his purpose, is to raise leaders. His passion is evident in line with his purpose.

Apostle Paul was also a man driven by divine purpose. Even when threatened by persecution and death, he refused to retreat but persisted in finishing his course.

Acts 20:24

"But I do not account my life of any value nor as precious to myself, **if only I may finish my course and the ministry** *that I received from the Lord Jesus, to testify to the gospel of the grace of God."*
(ESV)

4. It unlocks potential

Purpose helps maximize your potential. Potential is your unrealized capacity or ability. Your potential is determined by your purpose. An airplane has the potential to fly because that is its purpose, to transport in air. A train is not built with the potential to fly because its purpose is to travel by rail way.

The lack of knowledge of purpose leads to under performance. You cannot be productive while focusing on things outside your purpose. That is why many people do not realize their potential and they lack fulfillment in their life.

David as a young boy had the potential to be a leader and king of Israel. He needed to align himself with his purpose in order to realize his potential. Samuel helped reveal his destiny by anointing him as a young boy. This anointing was to prepare him to be king in the future.

1 Samuel 16:13

"Then Samuel took the horn of oil and **anointed him** *in the midst of his brothers. And the* **Spirit of the Lord rushed upon David** *from that day forward. And Samuel rose up and went to Ramah." (ESV)*

5. **It brings direction**

Purpose unlocks your vision and destiny in life. Direction is a function of vision and vision is birthed by purpose. Your purpose will birth a life vision of the desirable future you aim to achieve. This will give direction to your life as you begin to follow a certain path.

Without the understanding of purpose there is confusion and no clear direction of where to go. Gideon lacked direction because he did not know his purpose. His encounter with the angel of God transformed his life; he received a revelation of why he was born. He received divine purpose and direction for his life.

Judges 6:14

*"And the Lord turned to him and said, "**Go in this might of yours** and save Israel from the hand of Midian; **do not I send you?**" (ESV)*

6. It is ordained by God

Purpose is received from God; it is not something you can manufacture for yourself. God created you and He placed in you His purpose. God is purposeful in everything that He has created. Your purpose is divine, it has been ordained by God.

The responsibility to discover what God has ordained is with you. You have to make a deliberate decision to discover your purpose. It is too important to your life for you to leave it to chance. That is why I have written this book to help you on that journey. It is a joy for me to help you because it is my purpose to do that.

Jeremiah 1:5

*"Before I formed you **in the womb I knew you**, and before you were born **I consecrated you;** **I appointed** you a prophet to the nations."(ESV)*

7. **It is unchanging**

Purpose is not temporary, it is permanent. It is not like a job that one can change after some time, you cannot change your purpose.

God has purposed it and does not change His mind. It's no use trying to run away from your purpose, it is just a waste of time. The best thing you can do for yourself is to align with your divine purpose. The earlier you do it the better for you.

I have determined in my heart that l will strive to align my life with my purpose. Through God's grace, and help from mentors, I believe I am walking in my divine purpose. This has given meaning and direction to my life.

CHAPTER TWO
DISCOVER THE MIND OF GOD

Proverbs 20:5
*"The **purpose** in a man's **heart** is like **deep water**, but a man of **understanding will draw it out**."*
(ESV)

God has given every person a divine purpose. Our responsibility is to discover it and walk in it.

The first step to discovering your divine purpose is discovering the mind of God concerning your life.
God is the Creator of all things and He created them with purpose. Your purpose begins in the mind of God before it manifests in the physical realm. We have the responsibility to discover the mind of God, concerning our purpose. Before you were born you first existed in the mind of God, He planned your existence before you were born.

Jeremiah 1:5

"Before I formed you in the womb I knew you..."
(ESV)

DEFINING THE MIND OF GOD

1. God's thoughts

The mind of God means the thoughts God has about you. God has thoughts about your life, which is why He knew you before you were born. Parents do not start to think about their children after birth but before birth. I am a father of two children and I had thoughts about them before they were born. I continue to think about them as I see them grow up.

Psalm 139:17

*"How **precious** to me are **your thoughts, O God!** How **vast** is the sum of them!"*

Be assured that God had and has thoughts about your purpose. The thoughts of God about you reveal His mind concerning your purpose. You can find His thoughts about you in His word. His word reveals His general mind about you. Reading the Bible is a pathway to knowing the mind of God.

Isaiah 55:8
*"For **my thoughts** are not your thoughts,*
neither are your ways my ways, declares the Lord."
(ESV)

2. **God's plans**

The mind of God means the plans He has for you. There are plans God has made concerning your life. As parents, my wife and I usually make plans for our two children. The plans we make for them concerning their health, education, welfare etc, reveal our mind concerning them.

God has plans He has made for you, He has not left things to chance. Those plans reveal His mind concerning you. He has plans for your welfare, to give you a future and hope.

Jeremiah 29:11

*"For I know **the plans** I have for you, declares the Lord, **plans** for welfare and not for evil, to give you a future and a hope."* (ESV)

3. God's will

The mind of God means the will of God for you. The will of God speaks of the predetermined purpose of God. Everyone has a personal will but there is also the will of God. Often than not, these two are different. It is important to submit your personal will to the will of God. This is what Jesus did when he was praying in the garden of Gethsemane. He willingly submitted to the will of God to die on the cross, which was the opposite of His personal will.

The will of God can be categorized into two; the permissive will and the perfect will. The permissive will is what God will allow, even though it is not His best. Many times people are deceived to think they are in the perfect will because God has permitted certain things to happen. His perfect will is God's best for you. The paradox is that sometimes His best comes with pain and suffering, as in the case of Jesus Christ. Most people tend to run away from His perfect will to avoid the pain and difficulties. But they end up missing their divine purpose. The best place to live is in the perfect will of God. Let the prayer of Jesus be your regular prayer; *"not **my will** but **your will** be done"*. You need to learn to discern the will of God; it will lead you into discovering your purpose.

Romans 12:2
*"Do not be conformed to this world, but be transformed by the renewal of your mind, that by testing you may discern what is the **will of God**, what is good and acceptable and **perfect**."*
(ESV)

4. God's purpose

The mind of God means the purpose of God for you. His purpose means the reason why He created you. God has purposed things before creation. His mind is revealed in the reason why He created you. His purposes are eternal and unchanging. To Jeremiah He revealed His mind when

He told him that He purposed for him to be a prophet even before he was born. Your purpose is not an afterthought but it has been predetermined by God before you were born. God will align everything in your life according to His purpose for you.

Romans 8:28
*"And we know that for those who love God **all things work together** for good, for those who are called according to **his purpose.**" (ESV)*

5. **God's ways**

The mind of God means the ways of God in your life. The ways of God are His paths and processes. Every path leads to a specific destination, so in order to change your destination you have to change your path. When one follows the ways of God, they discover the mind of God concerning their purpose.

Isaiah 55:8
*"For my thoughts are not your thoughts,
neither are your ways **my ways**, declares the Lord."(ESV)*

STEPS TO DISCOVERING THE MIND OF GOD

There are steps you can take in order to discover the mind of God concerning your divine purpose. There are three key steps:

I. Accept Jesus as your Lord and Savior

You can only know the mind of God when you first accept Jesus as your Lord and Savior. We are all born in a fallen state of sin and sin separates us from God. Sin leads us contrary to our divine purpose. Before I surrendered my life to Jesus Christ, my life did not have meaning, it was full of confusion. Without Jesus people try and fill the gap with substitutes (money, marriage, fame, profession etc.) but they all fall short. The turning point for me was when I received Jesus and experienced the new birth. It was like scales were removed from my eyes and I began to view life from a clearer perspective.

Your divine purpose is in Jesus Christ, it is He that connects you to what God has originally purposed for you. Jesus Christ restores your relationship with God and He reveals God's plan for you. This is the most important step that begins the journey of discovering your purpose. Having received Jesus is just the start and not the end of the journey. Many people have been born again for years but are still far away from discovering and fulfilling their divine purpose. You need to make a conscious decision to pursue the journey of discovering your purpose.

Ephesians 2:10
*"For we are **his workmanship**, created **in Christ Jesus** for **good works**, which God **prepared beforehand**, that we should walk in them." (ESV)*

II. Reading and hearing the word

The mind of God has been revealed in His word contained in the Bible, it is the manual. Everything that is manufactured comes with a manual on how to use it correctly. When you buy a new gadget and you ignore the manual, you will misuse it and it will not last long. God did not leave us to guess work but gave us a manual which is the Bible. It is your responsibility to read the manual; it will guide you and help you avoid pitfalls that will destroy your life.

The word of God reveals to us, and empowers us for our divine purpose. Beyond reading the word, you need to listen to the preaching and teaching of the word. Many times when you read the manual there are things you will not understand, you need an instructor to explain with clarity. When you listen to the teaching and preaching of the word, you get more understanding concerning the mind of God about your purpose.

2 Timothy 3:16
*"**All scripture** is given by **inspiration of God**, and is profitable for doctrine, for reproof, for correction, for instruction in righteousness:" (KJV)*

III.   Pray for the Spirit to reveal God's mind

The Spirit of God knows the mind of God. God has given us the Holy Spirit to help us know the mind of God. That is why Jesus calls the Holy Spirit, "another helper." You have to ask Him to help you discover the mind of God for you. This should be one of your daily prayer requests.

1 Corinthians 2:10
*"These things God has **revealed** to us **through the Spirit**. For the **Spirit searches everything**, even the depths of God."*
(ESV)

The Holy Spirit helps us to discover the will of God and leads us in the path to discover our divine purpose.

Romans 8:27
*"And he who searches hearts knows what is the **mind of the Spirit**, because the **Spirit intercedes** for the saints **according to the will of God**."*
(ESV)

CHAPTER THREE
DISCOVER YOUR CALLING AND GIFTS

Romans 11:29

*"For the **gifts** and the **calling** of God are irrevocable."*

It was like I was experiencing labor pains; the burden of the call of God was so heavy upon me. From the time I surrendered my life to Jesus as an eighteen year old boy, I knew I was called. I did not fight it; I told God I am available whenever He needed me. I felt God was saying, *"I have to prepare you first"* So when I went to university I was mindful that God was preparing me.

I remember during my third year at university, when I was on work related learning; I told my parents that I have been called by God and in due season I will have to serve in ministry. They took heed and they prayed for me.

I completed my degree and started working. The awareness of the call of God upon my life gave me no rest and I did not know how to handle it. My struggle was mainly pertaining to these questions; *"when was it time for me to go into full time ministry and which ministry should I serve in?"* I took some time to pray and fast about it. The Lord directed me to go and see a certain Salvation Army Pastor. I set up an appointment and went to see him. I shared my story and experiences with him and I began to cry as I did. He took time to listen and then shared his experience on the journey of heeding the call of God. As he spoke I could relate and I got an understanding. He advised me to follow the leading of Spirit and that God would direct my path. That session greatly helped me to deal with the call of God upon my life.

I decided to attend Harvest House International Church Harare Bible School. This was a God ordained move. I enrolled for a Higher Diploma in Pastoral Studies and also Prophetic Studies. One of the modules on the Call of God was lectured by Reverend CS Tuturu. He shared his personal experiences of his struggles with the call of God. These lectures brought great understanding and clarity concerning the call of God. It was during one of the lectures, that God spoke to me and said, *"Go and serve under this man (Rev CS Tuturu)"*. Obeying that instruction aligned me with my calling and purpose, the rest, as they say, is history.

The second key to discovering our divine purpose is to discover our calling and gifts. God has called everyone but not everyone hears or responds to the call. Many people have made the calling of God mystical but it is not. God calls people according to His divine purpose.

Romans 8:28
*"And we know that for those who love God all things work together for good, for those who are **called according to his purpose**." (ESV)*

Once God has called you, He does not change his mind.

Romans 11:29
*"For the **gifts** and the **calling of God** are **irrevocable**." (ESV)*

DEFINING CALLING

To be called means the following three things:

1. **To be chosen**

To be called means that God has chosen you to be His vessel. It is God choosing you for a certain assignment. God can choose anyone, He is not a respecter of persons and He has no favorites. God chooses the very people the rest of the world would not consider because of their past failures and unfavorable backgrounds.

1 Corinthians 1:27
*"But **God chose** what is foolish in the world to shame the wise; **God chose** what is weak in the world to shame the strong;" (ESV)*

2. **To be invited**

To be called means that God has invited you to His divine plan. It is an invitation to be used by God according to His purpose. God invites many people but sadly many people give excuses for not honoring His invitation. He has invited you too; you need to accept His invitation.

Mathew 22:2-3

*"The kingdom of heaven may be compared to a king who gave a wedding feast for his son, and sent his servants to **call those** who were **invited** to the wedding feast, but they would not come."* *(ESV)*

3. To be set apart

To be called means that God has set you apart for an assignment. The calling of God will separate you from your friends and family. Many people reject the call of God because they do not want to be separated. All through the Bible the people God called, He separated them. Abraham was separated from his family and sent to a foreign land. The calling of God upon my life has led me to be assigned to work in a foreign country as missionary pastor, away from my family and friends.

Act 13:2

*"While they were worshiping the Lord and fasting, the Holy Spirit said, "**Set apart** for me Barnabas and Saul for the work to which I have **called them**."*
(ESV)

WAYS TO DISCOVER YOUR CALLING

1. Through serving

It is easier to direct something when in motion than when it is stationary. Many times people are inactive all in the name of "waiting for God to show them their ministry or calling". I remember at University, brethren were fascinated by what their and others' ministries were. God can better direct you towards your calling when you are active in the house of God. As you serve in God's house your calling begins to unfold.

Act 6:3

*"Therefore, brothers, pick out from among you seven men of good repute, full of the Spirit and of wisdom, whom we will **appoint to***

this duty."(ESV)

2. Through personal revelation

God can reveal your calling in the following ways:

I. God's voice

God still speaks today and you need to learn to hear His voice. Many times people think that God speaks with an audible voice; He does, but mostly He speaks to our spirit and to our mind. You have to learn to discern the Voice of God; it is usually a still small Voice. God will call you by His Voice, respond to His Voice.

1 Samuel 3:10-11
*"And the Lord came and stood, **calling** as at other times, "Samuel! Samuel!" And Samuel said, **"Speak, for your servant hears**. Then the Lord said to Samuel, "Behold, I am about to do a thing in Israel at which the two ears of everyone who hears it will tingle."*
(ESV)

II. Dreams and Visions

God also reveals your calling through dreams and visions. You need to take notice of your dreams because God calls people through their dreams. Not all dreams have a message from God but you need to be alert for dreams that carry a divine message. When I was in university I used to have dreams of myself standing in front and speaking to many people. God was showing me my calling to be a minister of the gospel.

Genesis 37:6-7
*"He said to them, "Hear this **dream** that I have **dreamed**: Behold, we were binding sheaves in the field, and behold, my sheaf arose and stood upright. And behold, your sheaves gathered around it and bowed down to my sheaf."*
(ESV)

III.   Prophetic words

God uses prophetic words to confirm your calling. The prophetic comes to confirm what God has already placed in your heart. It is also critical to be able to test prophecy using the standard of the word of God, in order to avoid being led astray. Over the years I have received a number of prophetic words that confirmed my calling however a few were misguided.

Act 9:17

"So Ananias departed and entered the house. And laying his hands on him he said, "Brother Saul, **the Lord Jesus who appeared to you on the road by which you came has sent me** *so that you may regain your sight and be filled with the Holy Spirit." (ESV)*

IV. Divine Encounters

God can also reveal your calling through a divine encounter. This is when God manifests Himself to you in a supernatural way. Gideon had an encounter with an angel. Not everyone is called in spectacular divine encounter like Paul; most people are called in an ordinary way.

Act 9:3

"Now as he went on his way, he approached Damascus, and **suddenly a light from heaven** *shone around him."* *(ESV)*

3. Through following

Another way to discover our calling is by following someone who mentors us. There are people that God has positioned in our lives to mentor and help us align with our purpose. Discovering these people I call "destiny mentors", is key to discovering your calling and gifts. They will guide you to realize your potential and discover your purpose.

One of my key destiny mentors that God used to align me with my calling was Reverend CS Tuturu. He saw the calling of God upon my life; he mentored and positioned me in line with my calling. Even if you are called by God and you know it, you cannot appoint yourself. Someone senior to you has to recognize the calling and appoint you. The challenge we have in this generation is self-appointed ministers. You cannot lay hands on yourself, fathers have to lay hands on you and set you apart into ministry. Even Paul who had a spectacular supernatural encounter had to be separated into his calling through the laying on of hands by fathers.

Many people confuse calling and commission. The two are separate events. There is a time gap between the two events, this gap is called preparation. When God calls you and you accept, the next stage is preparation. All people called by God went through a season of preparation before He commissioned them; Moses, David and Paul all went through the process of preparation. If you avoid the process of preparation you will be a half-baked vessel and you are likely to crack and fail in fulfilling your purpose.

DEFINING GIFTS

God has given everyone gifts in order to enable them to fulfill their calling and divine purpose. Gifts are given by grace according to one's calling. It is important to discover the dominant gifts in your life. There are three main categories of gifts in the scripture:

I. Motivational gifts

These are gifts available to everyone, but they differ according to grace. There are a total of seven motivational gifts. Every person has two or three dominant motivational gifts. You need to examine yourself and see which gifts operate in your life without struggle. Your dominant gifts are aligned with your area of calling and assignment.

Romans 12:6-8
*"Having **gifts** that **differ** according to the **grace given** to us, let us use them: if **prophecy**, in proportion to our faith; if **service**, in our serving; the one who **teaches**, in his teaching; the one who **exhorts**, in his exhortation; the one who **contributes**, in generosity; the one who **leads**, with zeal; the one who does acts of **mercy**, with cheerfulness."*
(ESV)

II. Spiritual gifts

Spiritual gifts are available to believers after the baptism of the Holy Spirit. There are nine spiritual gifts that are distributed as the Spirit wills. The scriptures encourage us to desire spiritual gifts. You cannot see the manifestation of spiritual gifts in your life unless you desire and pray for them.

1 Corinthians 12:1-11

"Now concerning spiritual gifts, brothers, I do not want you to be uninformed. You know that when you were pagans you were led astray to mute idols, however you were led. Therefore I want you to understand that no one speaking in the Spirit of God ever says "Jesus is accursed!" and no one can say "Jesus is Lord" except in the Holy Spirit. Now there are varieties of gifts, but the same Spirit; and there are varieties of service, but the same Lord; and there are varieties of activities, but it is the same God who empowers them all in everyone. To each is given the manifestation of the Spirit for the common good. For to one is given through the **Spirit the utterance of wisdom**, *and to another the* **utterance of knowledge** *according to the same Spirit, to another* **faith** *by the*

*same Spirit, to another **gifts of healing** by the one Spirit, to another the **working of miracles**, to another **prophecy**, to another the **ability to distinguish between spirits**, to another **various kinds of tongues**, to another the **interpretation of tongues**. All these are empowered by one and the same Spirit, who apportions to each one individually as he wills."*

III.   Ministry gifts

Ministry gifts are for the fivefold ministry offices. These ministry gifts are given by Jesus Christ to those He has set apart. There are five ministry gifts. Their purpose is to equip the saints for the work of ministry. When you develop your motivational and spiritual gifts, they will assist you when you are set apart for a specific ministry.

Ephesians 4:11
*"And he gave the **apostles**, the **prophets**, the **evangelists**, the **shepherds** and **teachers**,"*

KEYS TO DISCOVERING YOUR GIFTS

I. Self-examination

Examine yourself and check which gifts are operating in your life without struggle. You can also ask people around you to honestly tell you which gifts they notice in you. Once you discover your dominant gifts you have to work on developing them.

2 Corinthians 13:5

"***Examine*** *yourselves, to see whether you are in the faith. Test yourselves. Or do you not realize this about yourselves: that Jesus Christ is in you? —unless indeed you fail to meet the test!"*
(ESV)

II. Serving

Availing yourself to serve is a sure way to discover your gifts. If you are seated, not doing anything in the house of God, you will not discover your gifting. It is when you are active and serving that your gifting begins to manifest.

Act 6:3

"*Therefore, brothers, **pick out** from among you seven men of good repute, full of the Spirit and of wisdom, whom we will **appoint** to this **duty**.*"
(ESV)

III. Stirring

You have to put your gifts to use, if you neglect them they become dormant. You have to constantly stir your gifts and operate in them. Many people are gifted but look like they don't have any gifts because they hide their gifts and don't make use of them.

2 Timothy 1:6

"*Wherefore I put thee in remembrance that thou **stir** up the **gift of God**, which is in thee by the putting on of my hands.*"
(KJV)

God has called you to fulfill His divine purpose. In order to effectively fulfill that purpose, He has given you gifts. It is your responsibility to discover and utilize these gifts.

CHAPTER FOUR
DISCOVER YOUR TALENTS

Matthew 25:15

*"To one he gave five **talents**, to another two, to another one, to each **according to his ability**. Then he went away."*
(ESV)

The third key to walking in our divine purpose is to discover our talents. Everyone is born with talents and abilities. God has given you talents to help you fulfill your purpose. The talents you have are connected to your purpose.

Matthew 25:15

*"To one he gave five **talents**, to another two, to another one, to each according to his **ability**. Then he went away."*
(ESV)

The problem is many people do not discover and develop their talents. Some discover their talents, but do nothing about them, instead they bury their talents.

Matthew 25:25

"...so I was afraid, and I went and **hid** your talent in the ground. Here you have what is yours."
(ESV)

DEFINING TALENTS

1. **Natural abilities**

   Talents are the abilities to do certain things without much difficulty. For example, some people are naturally artistic. I know people who did not go to formal school to learn how to sculpture but they are naturally talented. You can enhance your natural ability through training.

   Exodus 31:3

   "...and I have filled him with the Spirit of God, with **ability** and intelligence, with knowledge and all **craftsmanship**," (ESV)

2. **Natural gifting**

   Talents are natural gifts we receive from God. There are people who are naturally gifted in athleticism, in organizing or singing. David's talent was in music and it is this gift that made room for him to go the palace and minister to King Saul. David's gift in music was connected to his purpose. To becoming the king who was a psalmist and he would establish the order of worship in the temple.

1 Chronicles 15:16

*"David also commanded the chiefs of the Levites to **appoint** their brothers as the **singers** who should **play** loudly on musical instruments, on harps and lyres and cymbals, to raise sounds of joy."*

3. **Natural skills**

Talents are natural skills that we develop. Some people have the skills to think logically or to play a musical instrument. When you develop your God given talent it becomes a skill. Daniel was given the ability to understand visions and dreams. He became skillful in this area and this led to his promotion in a foreign land, because he interpreted the dreams of the king of Babylon. Daniel's talent was connected to his purpose as a prophet. God would use him to intercede for the return of Israel to Jerusalem.

Daniel 1:17

*"As for these four youths, **God gave** them learning and **skill** in all literature and wisdom, and Daniel had **understanding** in all visions and dreams."*
(ESV)

KEYS TO DISCOVERING YOUR TALENTS

1. **Do a talent analysis**

   List the things you are able to do with little effort. Even if it looks insignificant it is still a talent. Do not look down on your talent. Can you imagine that years back no one thought making people laugh could be talent? Today there are people who are professional comedians, paid to make people laugh.

2. **Ask others the talents they see in you**

   Sometimes there are things you take for granted that others see as a talent. Ask a few close friends what abilities they see in you. You might be pleasantly surprised to discover the talents you might have overlooked. Not many people would see cooking as a talent but let me tell you people's ability when it comes to cooking differs. I do not have that talent but my wife has that talent yet she did not go to school to learn it.

The Colonel Sanders who started KFC in America years ago only had a special recipe to cook fried chicken. It is from that simple talent of frying chicken and being persistent after his recipe was turned down more than hundred times, but today we have KFC outlets worldwide. You might have eaten it too before, perhaps even be able to fry a more delicious chicken, the difference is how you perceive your ability to cook.

3. Get involved in an assignment

Your talents can only be exposed when you get involved in something. Volunteer to serve at your local church, at your school or at your workplace. You will never know what you are capable of until you do it.

HOW TO DEVELOP YOUR TALENTS

I. Preparation

Just having and knowing your talent is not enough. You have to set aside time to prepare and develop your talent. You have to prepare before opportunity manifests. When you fail to prepare you will not be able to maximize and excel using your talent. David had a talent of using a sling shoot and he would prepare alone in the wilderness. When the opportunity presented itself to fight Goliath, he was prepared for the challenge and he defeated Goliath. His small talent caused the whole nation to notice and he was made an army commander.

II. Practice

No matter how talented you are, you have to practice. Practicing helps to sharpen your talent, so that you become skillful. Many talented people are deceived to think that they do not need to work hard and that there is no need to practice. That is why many talented people do not live up to their potential. Look at someone as talented as Lionel Messi in soccer, every week he has to attend practice sessions under the instruction of a coach. Whatever talent you might have you need the discipline of practice in order to develop and nurture your talent.

III. Persistence

Results do not just manifest instantly, it takes time and process to produce desired results consistently. Talent alone does not guarantee desired results. You need to be persistent in putting effort. Being talented does not mean you avoid the process required and take short cuts. You need to be determined and not give up easily when faced with challenges.

Final word

The talents that you have are not just for display or decoration. God has given you those talents as tools to assist you in fulfilling your divine purpose. There are many talented people who are misusing their abilities for evil and harming others. That is why it is critical for you to discover your purpose in life, to enable you to utilize your talents in line with your divine purpose.

Some talented athletes have come to discover that their purpose is not being popular or rich but to use their talent to help others. At the time of writing this book; a footballer, who is the only African to be named FIFA footballer of the year, has been elected president of his country. Other talented footballers fail to find their purpose and become disoriented after their active playing career has ended. Your talent might be singing, writing or organizing. Whatever it is, without aligning with your divine purpose it is meaningless in the end. Determine to use your talents to fulfill your divine purpose.

CHAPTER FIVE
DISCOVER YOUR PASSION

Jeremiah 20:9
*"If I say, "I will not mention him, or speak any more in his name," there is **in my heart** as it were a **burning fire** shut up in my bones, and I am weary with holding it in, and I cannot."*

The fourth key to discover your divine purpose is discovering your passion. Everyone has something they are passionate about. Your passion is linked to your divine purpose. The passions have to be godly otherwise they will be evil passions that lead to distraction.

Jesus' passion was to do the will of God and to fulfill it. Speaking to His disciples, He likens His passion to food. He was willing to go without physical food because of His passion to do the work of God. When passion is directed in the right place, it is powerful. It is this passion that drove Jesus to the Cross, knowing He was going to suffer and die.

John 4:34

*"Jesus said to them, "**My food** is to do the **will of him** who sent me and to **accomplish his work**." (ESV)*

People are passionate about different things. Some of the things people are passionate about are:
- music
- technology
- children
- leadership
- business
- evangelism and
- sport

DEFINING PASSION

1. **Inner driving force**

Passion is a driving force that keeps you going, even in difficult times. When you do something you are not passionate about, you will easily give up when you are faced with challenges.

Paul was not preaching the gospel for personal gain but he was preaching out of passion. He was a man that was passionate about the gospel, even when beaten and left for dead he would continue to preach the gospel. Your passion should be connected to your purpose, so it becomes the inner driving force to fulfilling your purpose.

1 Corinthians 9:16

"For if I preach the gospel that gives me no ground for boasting. For **necessity** *is laid upon me.* **Woe to me** *if I do not preach the gospel!" (ESV)*

2. Intense commitment

Passion is an intense commitment to something. Passion releases a deep sense of commitment that is unwavering even in the face of obstacles. People of passion are people of commitment. They are committed to the cause and are willing to sacrifice anything for it.

Martin Luther King Jr. was passionate about equality for black people. He was committed to the cause that even when threatened with death he refused to back down. In one of his speeches titled 'Mountain top', he says, "I have seen the Promised Land and even if I don't get there. As a people we will get there…" A few days later he was assassinated. He was committed to his purpose unto death. Jesus is the ultimate example of this kind of commitment to death. He willingly offered Himself as a sacrifice to die on the cross, for the salvation of the world.

Hebrews 12:2

"…looking to Jesus, the founder and perfecter of our faith, who for the joy that was set before him **endured the cross***, despising the shame, and is seated at the right hand of the throne of God…"*
(ESV)

3. **Inner fire or zeal**

Passion is an inner zeal that motivates someone to action. People with passion are full of zeal, they are not passive. Passion is like fire that burns inside someone. Passion energizes people to pursue and do things that sometimes seem impossible. Jeremiah said; it was like fire shut up in his bones. Passion for your divine purpose can consume you to point where you have sleepless nights. There are times I am so consumed by the passion for my divine assignment that I cannot eat for some days and even have sleepless nights.

John 2:16-17

"And he told those who sold the pigeons, "Take these things away; do not make my Father's house, a house of trade." His disciples remembered that it was written, ***"Zeal*** *for your house will* ***consume*** *me."*
(ESV)

KEYS TO DISCOVER YOUR PASSIONS

I. Discover what you are willing to do without being paid

When you are passionate about something you are not motivated by money. Your passion is seen in things that you are willing to do without being paid. If you are called to minister the gospel, you should be passionate and willing to serve without being paid. The mystery is that people with this attitude, attract the blessing of God and prosper.

II. Discover what you are willing to die for

Passion for something inspires you to the state that you are willing to die for it. What is it that you willing to die for? When it comes to issues of sacrificing your life, it can only be something as important as your divine purpose that can motivate you.

III. Discover what moves you to sacrifice:

Whenever you are passionate about something, you are willing to sacrifice your time and resources for it. What are willing you to sacrifice your money and time for? Jesus said to His disciples, you can tell the heart of a person by where he invests or spends his money.

IV. Discover what is it you do with joy

When you are passionate about something, it brings you

joy to do it. What brings you great joy, even when you faced with difficult circumstances? Discovering and living in your purpose brings great joy and fulfillment. Joy is an internal state of wellbeing and gladness, it is long term.

IMPACT OF PASSION

I. Passion gives energy

People with passion have high energy levels. They are able to work hard for long hours without feeling exhausted. Their passion empowers them to keep going and pursuing their divine purpose.

II. Passion is infectious

People of passion have a positive effect on the people around them. They influence other people, inspiring and motivating them to achieve great things.

III. Passion transforms the atmosphere

People of passion transform a negative environment into a positive environment. They cause people to believe and change their mindsets.

People of purpose, are people of passion. Without passion to discover and fulfill your divine purpose, you will soon run out of steam. Refuse to be lukewarm but fired up with passion to walk in your divine purpose.

CHAPTER SIX
DISCOVER YOUR PLACE

Acts 17:26
*"From one man He has made every nationality to live over the whole earth and has **determined** their **appointed times** and the **boundaries** of where they live."*

The fifth key to discovering and walking in your divine purpose is to discover your place. For every divine purpose there is a place in which to fulfill it. You need to discover the place where your gifts and talents excel best. There is a place that God ordained for you to excel in your purpose. God has determined your time of existence and has set the boundaries of where you live. Remember you did not choose where to be born or which parents to be born to. It is God who has established your place of existence.

Matthew 10:5
"These twelve Jesus sent forth, and commanded them, saying, Go not into the way of the Gentiles, and into any city of the Samaritans

enter ye not:" (KJV)

DEFINING PLACE

a. **Geographical area**

Place means a certain geographical area you are assigned to fulfill your purpose. Your purpose has a certain area it is destined to make an impact in. It can be a city or country or region. Jesus' assigned place was in Judea and Galilee. He did not go out of region except once when he passed through Samaria.

Jesus had a clear understanding of His place, where He was going to fulfill his purpose. He decided to focus His ministry in his place. Jesus could have travelled to China or South Africa but He remained in His place of purpose. Even though He did not travel outside of Judea and Galilee, today His ministry on the cross has impacted every nation in the world.

Matthew 15:24
*"He answered, "I was **sent only** to the lost sheep of the **house of Israel**." (ESV)*

God can also stop you from going to certain places, which do not align to your purpose in that season.

Act 16:7
*"And when they had come up to Mysia, they **attempted to go** into Bithynia, but the Spirit of Jesus **did not allow** them."* (ESV)

b. Group of people

Your place can also mean a certain group of people. Every purpose has a specific target group of people. Discovering your place helps you know the group of people you are assigned to and where you will make the most impact.

Paul's ministry was mainly to the Gentiles and Peter's, to the Jews. When Paul began his ministry he tried to reach out to the Jews first but he was rejected. He later aligned with God's purpose to minister to the Gentiles and his ministry began to flourish and make a great impact.

Galatians 2:7

*"On the contrary, when they saw that I had been entrusted with the **gospel to the uncircumcised**, just as Peter had been entrusted with the gospel to the circumcised"*
(ESV)

Every person has their own target people they are called to. Some are called to work with young people, others with leaders, others with women and others with the less privileged.

c. **God's ordained spiritual house**

Place means a spiritual house that God has ordained for someone to be planted and to prosper there. Discovering your spiritual house is critical to discovering and fulfilling your divine purpose. A spiritual house means a church denomination or apostolic house. There is an Apostolic House that is your designated place to fulfill your purpose. You need to be planted in that house and not be jumping from house to house.

Paul discovered that his spiritual home was not Jerusalem

but the church at Antioch. In Damascus and Jerusalem Paul was rejected and his ministry was not accepted. It was when Barnabas brought him to the church in Antioch that he discovered his spiritual house and he was planted there. It was at Antioch that Paul's ministry began to develop and he was ordained as a missionary at Antioch. Wherever Paul travelled on his missionary journeys he would come back to Antioch and report back because that was his spiritual house or base.

Acts 13:1-3

"Now there were in the church at Antioch prophets and teachers, Barnabas, Simeon who was called Niger, Lucius of Cyrene, Manaen a lifelong friend of Herod the tetrarch, and **Saul***. While they were worshiping the Lord and fasting, the Holy Spirit said,* **"Set apart for me Barnabas and Saul** *for the work to which I have* **called them***." Then after fasting and praying they* **laid their hands** *on them and* **sent them** *off."*

KEYS TO DISCOVER YOUR PLACE

1. **Understand the geographical area of your purpose**

   Discovering the geographical area of your purpose requires prayer and seeking God. You have to be directed and led by the Holy Spirit. Reinhard Bonnke the German Pentecostal Evangelist's place is in Africa, it is the Holy Spirit who directed him as a young man to Lesotho. He did not just wake up and choose to go to Africa but he was led by the Holy Spirit. That is his place of his purpose and he prospered greatly there. Just a few months ago he had his farewell crusade in Nigeria, where he witnessed crowds of millions of people. Ever since God gave Evangelist Bonnke a vision for a blood-washed Africa – a continent washed in the blood of Jesus Christ – over 40 years ago, he has been filled with a burning commitment to win the continent for Jesus. Evangelist Bonnke has said, *"Whether I am eating or drinking, awake or asleep, the vision is ever-present. It never leaves me"*.

   Apostle Paul also depended on the Holy Spirit to direct him concerning where to go and minister. There are places he wanted to go and minister but the Holy Spirit did not allow him. He went where he was directed to minister and he aligned with his divine purpose.

Act 16:10

"And when Paul had seen the vision, immediately we **sought to go on into Macedonia,** *concluding that* **God had called us** *to preach the gospel to them."(ESV)*

2. **Realize the people who you are assigned to**

There is a need to discern the people you are called to minister to. You can minister to everyone but in order to be effective in your purpose, you have to discover a specific group you are called to minister to. Discovering and discerning this requires time.

Your purpose has a specific group of people that you are most effective and fruitful towards. As you relate with different people and follow God's leading you will soon discover the group of people you are called to. John Maxwell's place is to work mainly with leaders and that is where he puts his focus. Bishop Dag Heward-Mills' place is equipping and empowering Pastors. Mother Theresa's place was with helping the poor people of Kalkata in India.

Act 13:46

"And Paul and Barnabas spoke out boldly, saying, "It was necessary that the word of God be spoken first to you. Since you thrust it aside and judge yourselves unworthy of eternal life, behold, we are **turning to the Gentiles**.*"*
(ESV)

3. **Be planted in your ordained spiritual house**

There are many church denominations or apostolic houses but there is a specific place God has ordained for your purpose to flourish. It is your responsibility to discover this spiritual house and be planted there. There are people who shop around for churches like supermarkets; they end up confused and unfruitful. A tree that is planted and up rooted many times will not bear fruit. The secret to being fruitful is in abiding. You should not be casual about deciding which church to fellowship;

it is a destiny decision that needs to be taken prayerfully and purposefully. It's not that other churches are better than others but God has ordained your purpose to flourish in a certain church or apostolic house. The sooner you discover it the better you will align with your divine purpose.

Psalm 1:3

*"He is like a tree **planted** by streams of water that **yields** its fruit in its season, and its leaf does not wither. In all that he does, he **prospers**."*

WORD OF TESTIMONY

For me discovering the apostolic house in which to be planted was something I did not take for granted but considered very serious. I had the understanding that my divine purpose had a place God had ordained for it to flourish. I had been planted in my parents' church and after I was born again I remained there. I had prayed about this as a young boy and I sensed God was saying I should remain because He still had an assignment for me in my former church.

That proved to be true because the years that followed, I saw God use me (young as I was) to minister within the Church denomination as an instrument of revival. I thank God for many great encounters and meetings that I was privileged to be a part of. God opened doors for my preaching and prayer ministry to develop. I remember a territorial (national) youth congress that I had the honor of preaching at, it was God's doing because someone of my small rank did not get such platforms. I preached a message entitled: 'Restoration of Hope'. There was a great move of God that sparked revival among young people.

It was with this background that I was struggling with the call of God and asking God to direct me. Seated in a Bible School lecture, God spoke to me to go serve under Reverend CS Tuturu. This was a difficult instruction for me. I only knew Rev CS as a Bible School lecturer. I had been in my church denomination since I was born and my parents were senior leaders in Church. I was also encouraged with the great things God was doing in my former church and I had been assigned to lead young people at a local corps (assembly). I took time to pray and fast for weeks before I even shared this with my wife. I later shared with her and we began to pray about it together, until we had peace that God was leading us in that direction. We set an appointment to see Reverend CS Tuturu at his Church offices.

The day came and we went to see the man of God. He welcomed us pleasantly and we shared with him our story. He related to it well, even sharing with us his own story of how God called him and instructed him to leave his former church denomination, join and serve under Bishop Colin Nyathi. Bishop by then was a Pastor of a small Harvest House church in Bulawayo that was just about 2 years old. Reverend CS Tuturu then shared with us the church vision and advised us to go and be released by our Pastor before we could join a HHI local church in Harare.

We came out of that meeting with confirmation in our hearts that God was directing us to the right place, in line with our divine purpose. From there I set an appointment to see my parents and share with them the decision to move. It was a difficult decision for my parents but they understood and released me after praying for me. Thereafter, I wrote a letter to my Pastor explaining everything. He called us for a meeting and he also released us in the spirit of peace and understanding. We went to see Rev CS for the second time to update him and confirm that we were coming to join him. He took us out for lunch that day, what a blessing!

Now years later as I reflect on this I see that the hand of God was in this and He ordered our steps. Rev CS related to us years later that the first time we came to his office, God spoke to him that, "…this couple I have given you are Pastors, treat them well." Back then we were not Pastors at all, we were just ordinary members of the church. I remember the day we attended our first Harvest House International Church service in Harare my wife and I both felt we had found our spiritual home. God had aligned us with our calling and purpose as we were planted in HHI and served under Rev CS. The rest is history. My desire is to remain planted and serving because I believe there is more God has in store for us.

CHAPTER SEVEN
PURPOSE LED LIFE

Act 13:36
*"For David, after he had **served the purpose of God** in his **own generation**, fell asleep and was laid with his fathers and saw corruption,"*
(ESV)

Discovering your divine purpose is a journey not an event. It will not take a few days but years as it becomes clearer and clearer. The journey to discovering your divine purpose will transform your life. I strongly encourage you to start the journey. Lao Tzu says, "…the journey of a thousand miles begins with one step". This book is only a guide for that journey, you have to commit to discover and walk in your divine purpose.

As your divine purpose becomes clear, it's important to walk in it. You need to live a purpose-led life, where you pursue to fulfill your purpose daily. Life on earth is limited and we have to maximize every day given to us by

God. There are steps that can help one to live a purpose led life.

STEPS TO A PURPOSE LED LIFE

1. **Seek to do the will of God**

    Living a purpose-led life begins with seeking and doing the will of God. You should value the will of God above your own personal will. Let it be your priority to seek the will of God in your decisions and choices. Aim to live in God's perfect will for your life. It is the best place to live. Choose to obey the will of God even when it seems like it is the most difficult and painful option. The will of God is for your good and it will guide you into your divine purpose.

    John 4:34
    *"Jesus said to them, "**My food is to do the will of him who sent me** and to accomplish his work." (ESV)*

2. Accept and align with your calling

You need to accept and align to your calling as soon as possible. Rejecting and running away from your calling will only lead to frustration. The earlier you accept your calling, the earlier God begins to prepare and sharpen you. Do not allow past mistakes and failures to discourage you from accepting and believing that God can use you too. God specializes in using people that have been rejected by the world. Ask Moses who was rejected by his own people, a murderer and a fugitive but God still chose him and used him to deliver Israel.

Isaiah accepted his calling and availed himself to God. God is still asking; who can I send to do my purpose? I encourage you to avail yourself. Aligning with the call of God, will help you live a purpose led life.

Isaiah 6:8

"And I heard the voice of the Lord saying, **"Whom shall I send***, and who will go for us?" Then I said,* **"Here I am! Send me***." (ESV)*

3. **Serve faithfully in God's house**

Serving helps you align with your divine purpose. As you serve you discover your gifts and talents. A purpose led life, is a life of serving. God will order your steps better as you serve faithfully.

Every believer should serve faithfully in God's house. Philip was one of the seven deacons appointed in the early church, he served faithfully. God led him into his divine purpose as an evangelist.

Act 6:5
"And what they said pleased the whole gathering, and they **chose** *Stephen, a man full of faith and of the Holy Spirit, and* **Philip**, *and Prochorus, and Nicanor, and Timon, and Parmenas, and Nicolaus, a proselyte of Antioch."*
(ESV)

Act 8:4-8
"Now those who were scattered went about preaching the word. **Philip** *went down to the city of Samaria and* **proclaimed to them the Christ**. *And the crowds with one accord paid attention*

*to what was being said by **Philip**, when they **heard him and saw the signs** that he did. For unclean spirits, crying out with a loud voice, came out of many who had them, and many who were paralyzed or lame were healed. So there was much joy in that city."*

4. **Follow a destiny mentor**

Everyone has to discover and follow a mentor that will help them walk in their divine purpose. Destiny mentors stir your potential and build your capacity. As you follow a destiny mentor, you are led into your purpose. Not everyone you admire is your destiny mentor; you need be led by the Holy Spirit for you to recognise who your destiny mentor is.

Elisha discovered that Elijah was his destiny mentor and he made a decision to follow him. The decision to follow Elijah transformed his life and led him into his divine purpose. He was transformed from being a farmer into a Prophet.

1 Kings 19:20

"So he departed from there and found **Elisha the son of Shaphat,** *who was* **plowing with twelve yoke of oxen** *in front of him, and he was with the twelfth.* **Elijah passed by him and cast his cloak upon him.** *And he left the oxen and ran after Elijah and said, "Let me kiss my father and my mother, and then I will follow you." And he said to him, "Go back again, for what have I done to you?" And he returned from following him and took the yoke of oxen and sacrificed them and boiled their flesh with the yokes of the oxen and gave it to the people, and they ate.* **Then he arose and went after Elijah and assisted him.***" (ESV)*

5. Accept and excel at your assignment

Whatever the assignment that aligns with your purpose, you need to accept and excel in it. Along the journey of purpose, there will be various assignments that you will receive. Do not avoid these destiny assignments that God gives you. Some assignments look insignificant but they are crucial to you fulfilling your purpose.

David had various assignments that he had to carry out

and excel in on his journey to becoming king of Israel, which was his divine purpose. His first assignment was to take care of his father's sheep, then to take food to his brothers in battle. Accepting the second assignment led him to having the opportunity to fight Goliath, and his victory opened the door to elevation. Thereafter David had many other assignments that he accepted and excelled in before he was anointed king of Israel.

2 Samuel 7:8

"Now, therefore, thus you shall say to my **servant David***, 'Thus says the Lord of hosts, I took you* **from the pasture***, from following the sheep, that you should be* **prince over my people Israel.***"(ESV)*

6. Pursue your purpose with passion

You have to pursue your purpose with great passion. Unless you are passionate about discovering and walking in your divine purpose, you will give up easily. Do not allow your fire or zeal to be quenched by anything or anyone.

Apostle Paul remained passionate about fulfilling his purpose despite all the challenges he faced. The passion and zeal was like fire inside him that kept him going in the midst of persecution.

Act 20:22-24

"And now I am on my way to Jerusalem, bound in my spirit, not knowing what I will encounter there, except that in town after town the Holy Spirit testifies to me that chains and afflictions are waiting for me. **But I count my life of no value to myself, so that I may finish my course and the ministry** *I received from the Lord Jesus, to testify to the gospel of God's grace."*

Jeremiah 20:9

"If I say, "I will not mention him, or speak any more in his name," there is in my heart as it were a **burning fire shut up in my bones***, and I am weary with holding it in, and I cannot. (ESV)*

7. Utilize your gifts and talents

A purpose led life requires the full use of our gifts and

talents. Do not neglect your gifts or talents; they help you fulfill your divine purpose. Failure to use your gifts and maximize your potential will make it difficult for you to walk in your divine purpose.

Apostle Paul encouraged Timothy to fully utilize his gifts, in order to fulfill his ministry and purpose.

1 Timothy 4:14
*"**Do not neglect the gift you have**, which was given you by prophecy when the council of elders laid their hands on you." (ESV)*

2 Timothy 4:5
"As for you, always be sober-minded, endure suffering, **do the work of an evangelist, fulfill your ministry.***"*

FINAL WORD

It's time for you to discover and walk in your divine purpose. You were born for such a time as this; you have to serve the purpose of God in your own generation. David served the purpose of God in his generation and then he slept.

Acts 13:36
"For David, after he had served **the purpose of God in his own generation, fell asleep** *and was laid with his fathers and saw corruption,"(ESV)*

He was only ready to die after he had fulfilled his divine purpose. It is not acceptable for you to die before you have fulfilled the purpose of God. Arise and follow the example of David and Jesus Christ.

Hebrew 12:2
*"...***looking to Jesus***, the* **founder and perfecter of our faith***, who* **for the joy** *that was set before him* **endured the cross***, despising the shame, and is seated at the right hand of the throne of God."*

Jesus is our ultimate example of how to live a purpose led life. Let your focus be on Jesus Christ, His person, His principles and His power. My prayer for you; may the Holy Spirit guide you on this wonderful journey to discover and fulfill your divine purpose. Amen

REFERENCES & RECOMMENDED READINGS

i. **Bishop Colin Nyathi**, Desperate for God's Presence 2nd Edition, 2014

ii.

iii. **Rev Chemani Tuturu**, The House of Leadership, 2015

iv.

v. **Rev Chemani Tuturu**, Principles of Ministry, 2015

vi.

vii. **Rev Tonderai Mupamhanga**, Apostolic Mindsets and Paradigms, 2014

viii.

ix. **Dr Myles Munroe**, Understanding Your Potential, 1991

x.

xi. **Bishop Dag Heward Mills**, How You Can Be in the Perfect Will of God, 2011

xii.

xiii. **Rev Kenneth Hagin**, Plans, Purposes and Pursuits, 1988

DISCOVERING YOUR PURPOSE – BOOK REVIEW

One of the key outcomes I find in this book is bringing awareness to the reader about the great necessity to discover and pursue their purpose. Your purpose is everything to you – that's the very reason why you are on earth – to fulfill a purpose. What a tragedy it would be if we lived and never knew why we lived. Did you know that it is your responsibility to fulfill the purpose of God for your life? One of the common phrases these days is "YOLO" meaning "you only live once". At the end of your "one life", you will be required to answer the following simple but key questions:

- Did you fulfill your divine purpose?
- Did you fulfill the calling of God?
- Did you make maximum use of your talents?
- What legacy did you leave for generations after you?

While a good number of believers have an idea of why they are on earth, the vast majority aren't clear how to get there and hence they are likely to struggle to answer the above questions. They can see where they need to be, and they know that they are far from there. And every passing day they wonder how they will ever get there. Thank God for this brilliant book by Senior Pastor Matura, written in a simple, clear and easy to understand pattern.

The book lays out the need for the reader to identify and understand their divine purpose, calling, gifts, talents, passion and place. It further goes on to lay out practical keys to assist the reader to get there. This, coupled with Pastor Matura's own life experiences that every reader can easily relate to, infuses passion and a great desire to get going. This book is a practical, real life application tool in how to discover your divine purpose. I highly recommend it to the young who may be suffering from identity crisis, to the middle aged suffering from mid-life crisis and the aged who are facing the horizon of their lives.

I also recommend it to those who have discovered their purpose and are busy pursuing it; this book will certainly induce focus and passion necessary to keep you on track.

Thank you Pastor Matura for this exceptional master piece. Enjoy the book, and God bless you!

Pastor Learnmore Manhivi

www.ingramcontent.com/pod-product-compliance
Lightning Source LLC
Chambersburg PA
CBHW071310040426
42444CB00009B/1951